THE CRAFT OF
COCKTAILS

THE CRAFT OF COCKTAILS

Create the perfect cocktail

CONTENTS

CRAFT TECHNIQUES

To create the perfect craft cocktail, there are a number of techniques that you will need to master. As well as the basic mixology techniques that are essential for any bartender to grasp, there are artisan techniques such as infusion, seasoning, working with fire and ice, creating foams and airs, garnishing and decoration. Essential techniques are covered within the chapters so we look at infusing and flaming on pages 28–29, shaking and stirring on pages 56–57, building and layering on pages 92–93, muddling and blending on pages 122–123 and using bitters and sours on pages 156–157.

INFUSION

Infusion is everywhere in cocktail bars at the moment, from herb-, fruit- and vegetable-soaked spirits to liquors flavoured with such diverse ingredients as bacon, tea and woodchips. Infusions allow you to get really experimental and to create your own unique flavours – this kind of freedom is quite rare in mixology, which usually involves using ready-made ingredients in exact amounts, so it's great for the more creative cocktail mixer. In this book, there are lots of infused recipes, using a range of ingredients including rhubarb, peach, honey, ginger, green tea, beetroot and rosemary, but it's worth taking some time to test out some infusions of your own. If you like a particular herb or spice, try placing it with a favourite spirit in a sealed, sterilized jar for a week. Taste and see what you think of the flavour – if you want it to be stronger, simply seal and leave to infuse for another week or if it's too intense, then add more spirit to dilute the flavour. Another benefit of infusions is that you will always have ready-made flavoured spirits to hand, rather than having to muddle the ingredients together each time. The depth of flavour should also be stronger with infusions, depending on how long they've been left to mix.

SEASONING

People don't often think of adding seasoning to cocktails, but using some subtle flavourings can add a lot to the taste and depth of your alcoholic creations. Traditional seasonings include salt and pepper for cocktails such as the Bloody Mary, but modern mixologists are also using more complex flavours, such as herbs, spices, vinegars, chillies, hot sauces, horseradish and even barbecue sauces, to enhance their mixes.

The most common seasoning is salt and this can be either dissolved into the drink or added as a garnish (see page 12 for how to rim a glass with salt). As with food, a lot of drinks can be improved with a pinch or two of salt because it suppresses the bitterness of certain ingredients and enhances the flavours of others. Salt should be used sparingly though to avoid overwhelming the other ingredients. For Asian-themed drinks, a splash of soy sauce adds a salty, umami flavour and is especially good in smoky-flavoured cocktails. Ground black pepper works well in Bloody Marys and other savoury, rich cocktails.

Vinegars are used mainly in shrub cocktails (see pages 80–85) but can also be added to other drinks to create a tart, sharp flavour. The growing popularity of Kombucha-style drinks (fermented green or black teas) has added to the demand for vinegar flavours in cocktails and many bars now feature a variety of vinegar-seasoned drinks on their menus. Good types to use include balsamic, white or red wine, or sherry vinegars.

If you like spicy heat, you could experiment with using hot pepper sauce, chopped chillies, horseradish or wasabi paste in your cocktails.

TOOLS OF THE TRADE

GLASSES

Presentation is all in mixology, so it is important to serve a cocktail in the appropriate glass – the size, shape and style all have an impact on the visual perception and enjoyment of the drink. Here are some of the classic glasses that you will need to have in your collection.

MARTINI GLASS

The most iconic of all cocktail glasses, the conical martini glass emerged with the art deco movement. The long stem is perfect for chilled drinks as it keeps people's hands from inadvertently warming the cocktail.

HIGHBALL GLASS

Sometimes also known as a Collins glass, these glasses are perfect for serving drinks with a high proportion of mixer to spirit. The highball glass is versatile enough to be a substitute for the similarly shaped, but slightly larger, Collins glass.

LOWBALL GLASS

The lowball glass, also known as a rocks or old-fashioned glass, is a short, squat tumbler and is great for serving any spirit on the rocks or for short, mixed cocktails, such as the Old-Fashioned or Sazerac.

CHAMPAGNE FLUTE

The tall, thin flute's tapered design reduces the champagne's surface area and so helps to keep the fizz in the drink for longer. The flute has now largely replaced the coupe glass for serving champagne and champagne cocktails.

SHOT GLASS

This glass is a home-bar essential and can hold just enough spirit to be drunk in one mouthful. It also has a firm base that can be satisfyingly slammed on a bar top. The shot glass can also stand in for a measure when making cocktails.

COUPETTE GLASS

The coupette or Margarita glass was previously the traditional way to serve champagne, before the flute took over. Legend has it that the glass is modelled on a woman's breast. The coupette is now used to serve Margaritas and Daiquiris.

COUPE GLASS

Another wide-rimmed glass that is good for serving sparkling drinks. The short-stemmed coupe is also used for serving Daiquiris.

SNIFTER GLASS

The bowl-shaped snifter glass invites the drinker to cradle the drink in their hands, warming the contents of the glass, so is good for winter spirits, such as brandy. The aroma of the drink is held in the glass, allowing you to breathe in the drink before sipping.

HURRICANE GLASS

This pear-shaped glass pays homage to the hurricane lamp and was the glass used to create the New Orleans rum-based cocktail, Hurricane. It's also used for a variety of frozen and blended cocktails, such as the Piña Colada.

SLING GLASS

A variation on the highball glass, this is a design classic that is used to serve the Singapore Sling, the Long Island Ice Tea and the Mojito. Its tall body and short stem make it ideal for chilled drinks.

Introduction

MIXOLOGY KIT

What equipment you have in your home bar depends on whether you are the sort of person who likes all the latest gadgets or whether you are prepared to make do with the basics. Nowadays, there is no limit to the amount of bar equipment available, but you don't need lots of kit to make most of the drinks in this book. Here are some of the essential tools of the trade that you'll need.

MEASURES AND JIGGERS

A jigger is a bartender's basic measuring tool and essential for crafting the perfect blend of ingredients. Get a steel jigger with clear measurement markings so you can easily and accurately pour out measures.

BAR SPOON

A proper bar spoon has a small bowl and a long handle that allows you to muddle, mix and stir with ease. Spoons come in a variety of lengths and widths and a stylishly designed bar spoon is an attractive addition to any bartender's kit.

SHAKER

Most contemporary shakers are made from steel as they don't tarnish easily and they don't conduct heat easily – this is useful with chilled cocktails as the ice cools the cocktail rather than the shaker. Most standard shakers come with a built-in strainer, but if you're using a Boston or Parisian shaker then you'll need to use a separate strainer.

MIXING GLASS OR BEAKER

Any vessel that holds about 500 ml/1 pint of liquid can be used for mixing drinks. It is good to have a mixing glass with a spout or ridged rim so that you can stop ice from slipping into the glass, but this is not vital as a strainer can be used. Mixing beakers are increasingly popular nowadays and are usually made of glass or crystal.

MUDDLER

For mashing up citrus fruit or crushing herbs, you need a muddler. This is a chunky wooden tool with a rounded end and it can also be used to make cracked ice. You can do this job with a mortar and pestle but a muddler can be used directly in the mixing glass.

STRAINER

A bar or Hawthorne strainer is an essential tool to prevent ice and other ingredients being poured into your glass. Some cocktails need to be double strained so even if there is a strainer in your cocktail shaker, you'll still need a separate Hawthorne strainer in your bar collection.

JUICER

A traditional, ridged half-lemon shape on a saucer will work perfectly well for juicing small amounts. There is also a citrus spout that screws into a lemon or lime and is useful for obtaining tiny amounts of juice. Mechanical or electric presses are great for large amounts of juice, but not essential in a home bar.

OTHER EQUIPMENT

Other items you might need in your home-bar equipment are: corkscrew, bottle opener, cocktail sticks, blender, tongs, ice bucket, chopping board, knives, jugs, swizzle sticks, straws and an espuma gun for making foams.

Introduction

PREMIUM INGREDIENTS

SPIRITS

Stocking your bar with top quality spirits ensures that you are crafting your cocktails with the finest blends of flavours. A good bartender understands the strengths and aromas of each spirit and knows how to combine them with a variety of ingredients to bring out their flavours to the full.

WHISKEY: SCOTCH, IRISH, BOURBON AND RYE

Scotch whisky has been made since at least the 15th century and there are now over 100 distilleries in Scotland, with lots of small micro-distilleries springing up recently as well. There are two types of Scotch whisky: malt and grain. Malt whisky is made only from malted barley and grain whisky is made from malt and unmalted barley, as well as other grains. Single malt whiskies tend to be more expensive, although blended whiskies can be of excellent quality. Irish whiskey is similar to Scotch whisky, but Irish whiskey does not have the smokiness of Scotch. Irish whiskey tends to contain malted barley plus a wider range of grains.

Bourbon is a whiskey that is produced in the USA from a grain mash of not less than 51 per cent corn. It is a sour mash whiskey, which means that the spent mash left over from the previous fermentation is added to each new batch. Tennessee whiskey, such as Jack Daniels, is similar to bourbon but it is filtered through maple charcoal before it is aged.

Rye whiskey is mainly made in North America and is produced from a grain mash that is made up of at least 51 per cent rye grain. Rye whiskey is not as sweet as bourbon and tends to be slightly peppery.

VODKA

Vodka has its roots in Russia, Eastern Europe and Scandinavia and is a clear spirit with a neutral taste, making it excellent for cocktails. Vodka can be distilled from any plant that is high in sugar, such as potatoes, sugar beet or soya beans, although today vodka is normally made from a mash of grains, such as wheat, rye or corn, and is filtered through charcoal. How the vodka is distilled and how many times it is distilled are important factors in its quality and flavour.

GIN

Gin is distilled from any grain, potato or beet before being flavoured with juniper and other herbs and then redistilled. Gin got a bad reputation in England in the 18th century as it was so cheap that it was

more widely consumed than beer and was blamed for London's high death rate. Gin has seen a resurgence in recent years, with varieties such as sloe gin becoming more widely available.

RUM

Rum is strongly associated with the Caribbean, where it was first made in the 17th century. Rum is made by fermenting and distilling molasses to produce a clear liquid that is often aged in oak barrels or coloured with caramel to make dark rum. Rum can be turned into a liqueur and flavoured with fruit or coconut.

SCHNAPPS

Schnapps is a catch-all term for a spirit distilled from a grain or a fruit that is unsweetened. It is usually clear and has a neutral taste like vodka, so is often flavoured with fruits, such as peach.

TEQUILA AND MESCAL

Tequila and mescal are fermented and distilled from the agave plant that is grown throughout Mexico. Tequila is made from just the blue agave plant and only Mexico can legally produce this famous drink.

CACHAÇA

This is the national drink of Brazil and is an essential ingredient in the classic cocktail Caipirinha. This sugar cane spirit is the most popular distilled drink in Brazil.

ABSINTHE

Absinthe derives its name from the Latin for wormwood and is a spirit distilled from a mixture of bitter herbs, including wormwood, aniseed, angelica and cloves.

PASTIS, SAMBUCA AND OUZO

These are all aniseed-flavoured spirits that are often consumed as shots but can be used in cocktails to add a liquorice flavour.

SAKE

Sake is fermented rice wine that is clear and has a fairly neutral taste. There are many rituals involved with pouring and serving this drink in its native Japan.

Introduction

LIQUEURS AND WINES

Adding subtleties of flavour to cocktails can be easily achieved with the huge array of liqueurs and wines available. Whether you prefer your cocktails sweet or bitter, dry or sour, or short or long, having a wide range of liqueurs in your home bar is vital for any good mixologist.

BRANDY AND COGNAC

Brandy and cognac are distilled wines that are processed and then aged in oak barrels for between 2–10 years. Brandy was the first spirit to be sold globally and is the key ingredient for many classic cocktails. Cognac is a regionally specific brandy that is distilled twice, in comparison to most other brandies or Armagnac, which are distilled just once. Brandy has a caramel colour due to the ageing process in wooden casks and is usually drunk as an after-dinner digestif, as well as being a great base for many cocktails.

CHAMPAGNE

Champagne is the most famous wine-producing region in the world and is responsible for some of the most famous cocktails ever – the Champagne Sidecar and the Kir Royale, to name just two. Champagne is a drink that never seems to lose its style and despite other contenders to the fizzy wine crown, such as prosecco, cava or asti, champagne is still the sparkle of choice.

VERMOUTH

A fortified wine with a vital place in cocktail history – whether shaken or stirred, vermouth is an essential ingredient of the Martini. Vermouth comes in three types – red, bianco (or white), and dry, which is the type used in Martinis. It is made with a complex mix of herbs and spices that varies depending on the brand.

SHERRY

This Spanish fortified wine is made by combining brandy with wine and can range in flavour from very dry to very sweet dessert sherries. There are various types of sherry produced in different areas of Spain, such as pale cream, pale fino, light fino, Amontillado, Oloroso and pale cortado.

PORT

Originally exported from Porto in Portugal, from where it gets its name, port is a red wine that is fortified with brandy. It is very popular in the UK, where it is enjoyed as an after-dinner digestif and often partnered with cheese. Vintage port tends to be unfiltered, so it needs to be decanted to remove the sediment.

AMARETTO

A golden-brown Italian liqueur with a bitter-sweet almond taste. Its distinctive flavour comes from being made with burnt sugar and up to 17 herbs and fruits.

TRIPLE SEC, GRAND MARNIER, CURAÇAO AND COINTREAU

These are all orange-flavoured liqueurs and are used in many cocktails to give a sweet, citrus taste.

SOUTHERN COMFORT

A brand of American whiskey-based liqueur that is flavoured with peach brandy, orange, vanilla and cinnamon.

IRISH CREAM

A whiskey-based liqueur, its creamy flavour makes it a great base for more decadent, after-dinner cocktails.

Introduction

MIXERS AND FLAVOURINGS

As wonderful as alcohol is, you will also need to stock your home bar with a good range of mixers and flavourings in order to mix up a range of cocktails. The balance of alcohol to mixer is vital in achieving that unique flavour so ensure you have all the essential mixers in your collection.

SODA WATER

Soda water is similar to fizzy mineral water, but it has added salts, such as sodium bicarbonate. It is a neutral mixer that is useful for creating long cocktails without adding too much additional flavour.

TONIC WATER

A carbonated water that contains a small amount of quinine, tonic water gives cocktails a slightly bitter taste and is good with simple spirits such as vodka and gin.

COLA

Cola has a complex mix of flavours that brings a lot to a cocktail, with hints of lemon, orange, lime, cinnamon, lavender, coriander and nutmeg. This allows it to be used with quite simple ingredients to produce a still flavourful drink – for example, the classic Cuba Libre is just rum, cola and lime.
Cola works best with rum or whiskey, but is also good with neutral-tasting vodka.

GINGER BEER

Dating back to the 18th century, ginger beer is slightly fizzy and, in its naturally fermented state, very mildly alcoholic. Its basic ingredients are ginger, lemon, sugar and a fermenting ingredient, such as yeast. It is used in the famous cocktail Moscow Mule and combines well with vodka.

GINGER ALE

Ginger ale is a carbonated soft drink that is similar to ginger beer but with a much subtler ginger flavour. It is also clear rather than cloudy and has a dry flavour that works well in cocktails.

LEMONADE

Shop-bought lemonade is a clear, fizzy carbonated drink flavoured with lemon and lime. This style of lemonade is the type to use in cocktails, as opposed to traditional lemonade, which has more of a citrus hit but is too overpowering for most drinks.

BITTER LEMON

Bitter lemon is tonic water flavoured with lemon. The signature bitter taste is produced by the combination of the quinine and the lemon pith used to make this drink.

FRUIT JUICE

Shop-bought or home-squeezed juices are both fine to use in cocktails, although home-produced juices will need to be strained to remove any bits. Orange juice goes well with

vodka and tequila, pineapple juice is good with rum, and cranberry juice combines perfectly with vodka.

SUGAR SYRUP

This combination of sugar and water is used to sweeten drinks. To make home-made sugar syrup, bring 2 measures of water to the boil in a saucepan. Remove from the heat and add 1 measure of sugar, stirring to dissolve. Leave to cool then pour into a bottle and refrigerate. This will keep for up to 1 month in the fridge. Quantities can be scaled up if more sugar syrup is needed.

ANGOSTURA BITTERS

Less of a mixer and more of a flavour enhancer, Angostura bitters is made from a secret blend of herbs and spices. Despite its name, it isn't bitter when added to a drink but has the ability to bring out the flavour of the other ingredients.

GRENADINE

Grenadine is a non-alcoholic, pomegranate-flavoured syrup that is used to sweeten cocktails and to colour them pink or red.

SPECIALIST SPICES

For some of the recipes in this book, you will need to buy some more specialist herbs and spices. For example, to make your own homemade gin on page 42, you will need juniper berries, angelica root, orris root and liquorice root.

INFUSING & FLAMING

INFUSING & FLAMING

Infusions are a fantastic way to introduce some creative flair to your cocktail making – you can combine spirits and flavours to produce some inventive new ingredients that you can use again and again in your mixology. In this chapter, we use a variety of infusion techniques – from the simple method of combining spirits and ingredients in a jar for a period of time to creating fruit-infused syrups to add to your drinks. We also feature on-trend ingredients, such as matcha green tea and smoky bacon, to create some truly inventive, up-to-the-minute craft cocktails. For more on creating your own infusions, see page 8.

Flaming drinks are an eye-catching addition to any party or evening with friends, and, as well as looking impressive, igniting your drink can actually enhance the flavour. Lit drinks can be as simple as a flaming shooter or as dramatic as an on-fire punch bowl, but remember: when serving even the most basic flaming shot, dim the lights for the full fiery effect. For flaming drinks, you'll need to use an ignition agent – in this chapter, we use 151 rum as the alcohol level is very high but any spirit that is at least 80 per cent proof is fine to use. It is important to follow the amount specified in the recipes as using too much flaming agent could be dangerous. For more on lighting your cocktails and for advice on fire safety, see page 10.

RHUBARB & VANILLA BOURBON COCKTAIL

SERVES 1

INGREDIENTS

1 vanilla pod, halved and seeds scraped

200 g/7 oz fresh rhubarb, chopped

50 g/1¾ oz sugar

2 tbsp grenadine

350 ml/12 fl oz bourbon

whole ice cubes

½ measure lemon juice

175 ml/6 fl oz pear juice

sliver of vanilla pod, to decorate

TIP

You could also try infusing the rhubarb with vodka, gin or rum, but make sure you add the grenadine as this adds a nice pink tone.

1.
This cocktail takes 1 week to infuse. Put the pod and seeds in a saucepan. Add the rhubarb and place over a low heat. Add the sugar and simmer for 5 minutes, or until softened. Stir.

2.
Leave to cool. Place the mixture in a sterilized, sealable jar and add the grenadine and bourbon. Keep the bourbon bottle for later use. Mix and seal. Leave in a cool place for 1 week.

3.
After 1 week, pour the bourbon mixture through a fine sieve and strain through a coffee filter. Place 2 measures of the bourbon into a shaker (any remaining bourbon can be stored for up to 2 months). Add some ice, the lemon and pear juice and shake vigorously until well frosted. Fill a highball glass with ice cubes and strain the cocktail into the glass. Decorate with vanilla and serve immediately.

HONEY, PEACH & AGAVE INFUSION

SERVES 1

INGREDIENTS

2 ripe peaches, cut into wedges

10 peppercorns

2 star anise

½ vanilla pod, split

1 cinnamon stick

2 tbsp agave syrup

2 tbsp honey

350 ml/12 fl oz tequila

whole ice cubes

1 measure rum

1 measure lime juice

1 egg white

1 measure triple sec

peach slice, to decorate

TIP

For an alternative flavour, try using a combination of soft fruits such as nectarines, plums and apricots, instead of peaches.

1.
This cocktail takes 1 month to infuse. Place the peach wedges in a sterilized, sealable jar. Add the peppercorns, star anise, vanilla, cinnamon, agave, honey and tequila. Keep the tequila bottle for later use.

2.
Mix and seal. Leave in a cool place for 1 month. After 1 month, strain the tequila through a fine sieve. Once strained, pour the tequila back into its bottle. Place 1 measure of the tequila into an ice-filled cocktail shaker. The rest of the tequila can be stored for up to 2 months. Add the rum, lime juice, egg white and triple sec.

3.
Shake vigorously until well frosted. Strain into an ice-filled lowball glass and decorate with the peach slice. Serve immediately.

PLuM & GiNGER WHISKEY FIZZ

SERVES 1

INGREDIENTS

6 ripe plums, roughly chopped

large piece of fresh ginger, peeled and sliced

2 tbsp granulated sugar

3 whole cloves

350 ml/12 fl oz whiskey

whole ice cubes

1 measure lemon juice

175 ml/6 fl oz soda water

lemon slice, to decorate

TIP
This would make a great drink to start off a cocktail party, guaranteed to create a party atmosphere.

1.
This cocktail takes 1 week to infuse. Place the plums, ginger, sugar and cloves into a saucepan. Place over a low heat and cook for 5 minutes. Leave to cool. Place the mixture into a sterilized, sealable jar. Add the whiskey and mix. Keep the whiskey bottle for later use. Seal and leave in a cool place for 1 week.

2.
After 1 week, pour the whiskey through a fine sieve and then strain through a coffee filter. Once strained, pour the whiskey back into its bottle. Place 2 measures of the whiskey into an ice-filled cocktail shaker. The rest of the whiskey can be stored and used for up to 2 months. Add the lemon juice to the cocktail shaker. Shake vigorously until well frosted, then pour into an ice-filled highball glass. Top up with soda water and decorate with a lemon slice. Serve immediately.

PEACH & BASIL GIN FIX

SERVES 1

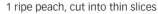

INGREDIENTS

1 ripe peach, cut into thin slices

125 ml/4 fl oz water

100 g/3½ oz caster sugar

12 basil leaves

crushed ice

2 measures gin

¾ measure lemon juice

peach slices and basil leaves,
to decorate (optional)

TIP

For a classic gin fix, omit the peach
and basil when making the syrup.

1.
Place the peach slices, water and
sugar into a saucepan and bring to
the boil over a high heat. Add the
basil leaves then remove from the
heat and leave to cool. Once cooled,
strain the liquid through a fine sieve
and store in a sterilized, sealable jar.

2.
Fill a lowball glass with crushed ice.
Add 1 measure of the peach-infused
syrup to the glass and then add the
gin and lemon juice. Any remaining
syrup should be stored in the
refrigerator and used within 1 week.

3.
Stir well and decorate the glass with
the peach slices and basil leaves, if
using. Serve immediately.

Infusing & Flaming

MATCHA GREEN TEA VODKA REFRESHER

SERVES 1

INGREDIENTS

350 ml/12 fl oz vodka

1 tsp matcha green tea powder

2 small cinnamon sticks

whole ice cubes

1 tsp honey

¼ measure lemon juice

1 measure cloudy apple juice

1 small cinnamon stick, to decorate

TIP
This refreshing drink is a good way to start off a Friday evening as you wind down for the weekend.

1.
This cocktail takes 24 hours to infuse. Pour the vodka into a sterilized, sealable jar. Keep the vodka bottle for later use. Add the green tea and the cinnamon sticks. Mix then seal and leave in a cool place for 24 hours.

2.
After 24 hours, remove the cinnamon and strain through a coffee filter. Pour the infused vodka back into its bottle.

3.
Chill a coupe glass. Put 2 measures of the infused vodka into an ice-filled cocktail shaker. The rest of the vodka can be stored for up to 2 months. Add the honey, lemon and apple juice.

4.
Shake vigorously until well frosted and then strain the cocktail into the glass. Decorate with the cinnamon stick and serve immediately.

BEETROOT VIRGIN MARY

SERVES 1

INGREDIENTS

30 g/1 oz raw beetroot, peeled

175 ml/6 fl oz tomato juice

1 tsp Worcestershire sauce

¼ tsp celery salt

¼ tsp pepper

1 tsp freshly grated horseradish

½ tsp hot pepper sauce

whole ice cubes

1 lemon slice, to decorate

celery stick, to decorate

TIP

If you're feeling adventurous, try swapping the tomato juice for Clamato juice and add your favourite fiery hot sauce!

1.
Cut the beetroot into small pieces. Place in a cocktail shaker and crush thoroughly with a muddler or pestle to release the colour and flavour.

2.
Add the tomato juice, Worcestershire sauce, celery salt, pepper, horseradish and hot pepper sauce. Stir well with a bar spoon.

3.
Pour the mixture into a Collins or highball glass.

4.
Add some ice cubes and stir again.

5.
Decorate the drink with the lemon slice and celery stick. Serve immediately.

HOMEMADE GIN

MAKES 750 ML/1¼ PINTS

INGREDIENTS

700 ml/1¼ pints vodka

20 juniper berries

2 g/¹⁄₁₆ oz angelica root

2 g/¹⁄₁₆ oz orris root

8 g/¼ oz coriander seeds

2 g/¹⁄₁₆ oz liquorice root

2 g/¹⁄₁₆ oz orange peel

2 g/¹⁄₁₆ oz lemon peel

TIP
For alternative flavours, you can also add other ingredients, such as cardamom pods, cassia bark, ginger root, rose petals and nutmeg, to give it your own twist.

1.
This cocktail takes 48 hours to infuse. Pour the vodka and all the ingredients, except the orange and lemon peel, into a sterilized, sealable jar. Keep the vodka bottle for later use. Seal the jar and leave to infuse for 24 hours.

2.
Add the orange and lemon peel and leave to infuse for a further 24 hours. The reason for adding the peels later is to keep the citrus notes fresh and to stop it from becoming too bitter.

3.
Strain the mixture through a sieve and then strain again through a muslin.

4.
Pour back into the vodka bottle and serve when needed.

ROSEMARY VODKA COOLER

SERVES 1

INGREDIENTS

350 ml/12 fl oz vodka

2 sprigs of rosemary

whole ice cubes

½ measure sugar syrup

½ measure lime juice

150 ml/5 fl oz ginger beer

rosemary sprigs and lime slices,
to decorate

TIP
For an extra ginger hit, replace the
rosemary with 55 g/2 oz of freshly
sliced ginger.

1.
This cocktail takes 1 week to infuse.
Place the vodka in a sterilized, sealable
bottle or jar and add the rosemary
sprigs. Seal and leave to infuse for
1 week.

2.
Once infused, put 2 two measures of
the rosemary vodka in an ice-filled
Collins or highball glass.

3.
Add the sugar syrup and lime juice to
the glass. Top up with the ginger beer
and stir.

4.
Decorate with the rosemary and lime
slices. Serve immediately.

BACON & MAPLE COCKTAIL

SERVES 1

INGREDIENTS

200 g/7 oz good quality smoked bacon

350 ml/12 fl oz bourbon

whole ice cubes

1 measure apple brandy

1 measure maple syrup

1 measure fresh lemon juice

1 egg white

¼ tsp mixed spice

1.
This cocktail takes 2–3 days to infuse. Place a frying pan over a medium heat and add the bacon. Fry for 5 minutes, or until the fat has melted. Carefully strain the bacon fat through a fine sieve into a bowl and leave to cool slightly. Set aside the bacon.

2.
Pour the fat into a sterilized, sealable jar. Add the bourbon and seal. Shake vigorously for a few seconds then place in a refrigerator for 2–3 days. Make a hole in the fat with a spoon. Strain the bourbon through muslin back into its bottle. Place ice cubes into a cocktail shaker. Pour over 1 measure of the bourbon, the apple brandy, maple syrup, lemon juice and egg white. Shake until well frosted. The rest of the bourbon can be stored for up to 2 months. Strain into a lowball glass filled with ice. Dust with the spice and serve immediately.

Infusing & Flaming

CiDER & RASPBERRY SLUSHiE

SERVES 1

INGREDIENTS

500 ml/18 fl oz cider

150 g/5½ oz fresh raspberries,
plus 2 to decorate

TIP
For a non-alcoholic version of this,
try using lemonade instead of cider
and experiment with different berries
such as blackberries, strawberries
or blueberries.

1.
Pour the cider into a freezerproof
plastic container with a lid.

2.
Secure the container with the lid and
place in the freezer for 3 hours, or until
the cider has frozen.

3.
Remove the cider from the freezer and
break up the mixture with a fork, until
the cider is in small chunks.

4.
Put the raspberries in a blender with
the cider chunks and blend until you
have a slushie consistency.

5.
Serve immediately in a pint glass with
a straw and decorate with the fresh
raspberries.

Infusing & Flaming

HAZELNUT VODKA ESPRESSO

SERVES 1

INGREDIENTS

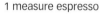

1 measure espresso
2 measures Frangelico
½ measure vodka
½ tsp caster sugar
whole ice cubes
1 marshmallow
½ measure 151 rum

TIP
This is a luxurious after-dinner treat –
just turn down the lights and serve
it flaming!

1.
Pour the espresso, Frangelico,
vodka and sugar into an ice-filled
cocktail shaker.

2.
Shake vigorously until well frosted.
Strain into a heatproof coupe or
coupette glass.

3.
Place the marshmallow on top of the
cocktail. Gently pour the 151 rum
over the marshmallow.

4.
Set the marshmallow alight using
a long match, then allow the flames
to die down completely and check
the marshmallow and glass have
cooled before drinking.

FLAMING CUCUMBER SAKE

SERVES 1

INGREDIENTS

1 small cucumber, thinly sliced
350 ml/12 fl oz sake
10 peppercorns
1 long, thin cucumber slice
whole ice cubes
1 measure vodka
½ measure lime juice
1 measure sugar syrup
½ measure 151 rum

1.
This cocktail takes 24 hours to infuse. Place the cucumber, sake and peppercorns in a sterilized, sealable jar. Seal and leave in a cool place for 24 hours. Keep the sake bottle for later use.

2.
Strain the sake through a fine sieve. Once strained, pour the sake back into its bottle.

3.
Place the cucumber slice around the inside of a heatproof lowball glass. Add a few ice cubes to the glass. Pour 1 measure of the infused sake, the vodka, lime juice and sugar syrup into a ice-filled cocktail shaker. The rest of the sake can be stored and used for up to 2 months.

4.
Shake vigorously until well frosted. Strain into the glass. Gently pour the 151 rum into the glass over the back of a teaspoon, so it sits on top of the drink. Set alight using a long match, then allow the flames to die down and the drink to cool completely before drinking.

FLAMING MAI TAI

SERVES 1

1.
Place the ice cubes into a cocktail shaker. Pour over the rum, triple sec, brandy, pineapple juice and almond syrup.

2.
Shake vigorously until well frosted. Fill a heatproof hurricane glass with ice cubes then strain the cocktail into the glass.

3.
Place the chopped pineapple, cinnamon and 151 rum into a mixing glass. Stir with a bar spoon to combine.

4.
Tilt the mixing glass and light the rum mixture with a long match. With care and using flame-resistant gloves, pour the lit rum mixture into the cocktail in the hurricane glass.

5.
Allow the flames to die down and the drink to cool completely before drinking. Decorate with mint leaves and serve.

INGREDIENTS

whole ice cubes
1 measure brown rum
½ measure triple sec
½ measure brandy
125 ml/4 fl oz pineapple juice
½ measure almond syrup
55 g/2 oz chopped fresh pineapple
½ tsp cinnamon
½ measure 151 rum
mint leaves, to decorate

SHAKING & STIRRING

SHAKING & STIRRING

These are the two most basic mixology techniques, but they are essential to master in order to confidently make a range of both classic and craft cocktails. Shaking is when you add all of the ingredients, with the specified amount of ice cubes, to the shaker and then shake vigorously for approximately 5–10 seconds. The benefits of shaking are that the drink is rapidly mixed, chilled and aerated. Once the drink has been shaken, the outside of the shaker should be lightly frosted.

Shaking a cocktail also dilutes the drink quite significantly. This dilution is an essential part of the cocktail-making process and gives shaken recipes the correct balance of taste, strength and temperature. The drink is then double strained into glasses – the shaker should have an inbuilt strainer and you usually use a separate strainer over the glass as well. Shaking can also be used to prepare cocktails that include an ingredient, such as an egg white, that will not combine with less vigorous forms of mixing.

Stirring is the purist's choice – it's where you add all the ingredients, usually with some ice cubes, but this time you combine them in a mixing glass or beaker and then stir the ingredients together using a long-handled bar spoon or swizzle stick. As with shaking, this allows you to blend and chill the ingredients without too much erosion of the ice, so you can control the level of dilution and keep it to a minimum. This simple technique is vital for drinks that do not need a lot of dilution, such as the classic Dry Martini.

TURKiSH DELiGHT GiN CoCKTAiL

SERVES 1

INGREDIENTS

2 measures gin

175 ml/6 fl oz cranberry juice

1 tbsp honey

¼ tsp rosewater

a few ice cubes

1 tbsp pomegranate seeds

¼ tsp dried rose petals, plus extra
to decorate

TIP
If you really love a floral taste, try
using lavender petals instead of rose
petals and lavender honey instead of
normal honey.

1.
Pour the gin, cranberry juice, honey
and rosewater into a Collins or
highball glass.

2.
Stir with a bar spoon until the honey
has dissolved.

3.
Add the ice cubes, pomegranate seeds
and rose petals, then stir again.

4.
Decorate with the rose petals and
serve immediately with a straw.

BOULEVARDIER

SERVES 1

1.
Place the ice cubes into a cocktail shaker.

2.
Pour over the bourbon, vermouth and Campari, then stir well with a bar spoon.

3.
Strain the cocktail into a chilled coupe or coupette glass.

4.
Decorate with the lemon twist and serve immediately.

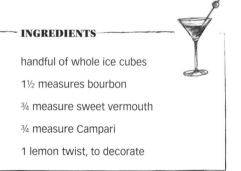

INGREDIENTS

handful of whole ice cubes

1½ measures bourbon

¾ measure sweet vermouth

¾ measure Campari

1 lemon twist, to decorate

MANHATTAN

1.
Put the cracked ice cubes into a cocktail shaker.

2.
Pour the liquid ingredients over the ice cubes.

3.
Shake vigorously until well frosted.

4.
Strain into a chilled martini glass and decorate with the cherry. Serve immediately.

INGREDIENTS

4–6 cracked ice cubes

1 tsp Angostura bitters

3 measures rye whiskey

1 measure sweet vermouth

cocktail cherry, to decorate

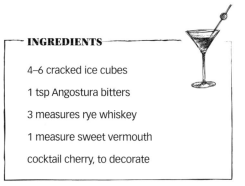

WHISKEY SLING

1.
Put the sugar into a mixing glass.

2.
Add the lemon juice and water and stir until the sugar has dissolved.

3.
Pour in the whiskey and stir to mix.

4.
Half-fill a small chilled lowball glass with cracked ice and strain the cocktail over it. Decorate with the orange wedge. Serve immediately.

INGREDIENTS

1 tsp icing sugar

1 measure lemon juice

1 tsp water

2 measures American blended whiskey

cracked ice cubes

orange wedge, to decorate

MARGARITA

SERVES 1

INGREDIENTS

2 lime wedges

coarse salt

4–6 cracked ice cubes

3 measures white tequila

1 measure triple sec

2 measures lime juice

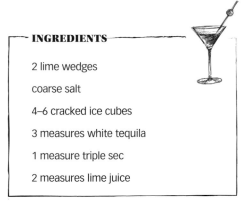

1.
Rub the rim of a chilled martini glass with a lime wedge.

2.
Dip the rim in a saucer of coarse salt.

3.
Put the cracked ice cubes into a cocktail shaker. Pour over the tequila, triple sec and lime juice and shake vigorously until well frosted. Strain into the glass.

4.
Decorate with the remaining lime wedge. Serve immediately.

GIN RICKEY

1.
Fill a chilled highball glass or goblet with cracked ice.

2.
Pour over the gin and lime juice. Top up with the soda water.

3.
Stir gently to mix and decorate with a lemon slice. Serve immediately.

INGREDIENTS

cracked ice cubes

2 measures gin

1 measure lime juice

soda water

lemon slice, to decorate

MARTINI

SERVES 1

1.
Put the cracked ice cubes into a cocktail shaker.

2.
Pour the gin and vermouth over the ice cubes.

3.
Shake until well frosted. Strain into a chilled martini glass.

4.
Decorate with the olive. Serve immediately.

INGREDIENTS

4–6 cracked ice cubes

3 measures gin

1 tsp dry vermouth, or to taste

cocktail olive, to decorate

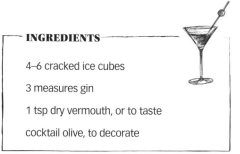

RUM COBBLER

SERVES 1

INGREDIENTS

100 g/3½ oz whisky-barrel woodchips

350 ml/12 fl oz brown rum

crushed ice

splash of grenadine

½ measure maraschino liqueur

maraschino cherry, orange slices and
lime slices, to decorate

TIP
For a variation of this drink, substitute
one of the measures of rum with port
and add a splash of pineapple juice.

1.
This cocktail takes 2 weeks to infuse
and you will need a blowtorch. Lay the
whisky-barrel chips on a metal tray
and place on a heatproof surface.

2.
Using a blowtorch, scorch all over
the woodchips until about half
have blackened. Put the scorched
woodchips into a sterilized, sealable
jar, then pour in the rum. Keep the rum
bottle for later use. Mix and seal the jar.
Leave in a cool place for 2 weeks.

3.
After 2 weeks, strain the rum through
a fine sieve. Fill a lowball glass with
ice. Pour in 2 measures of the rum. The
rest can be stored for up to 2 months.

4.
Add the grenadine and maraschino
and stir. Decorate with the cherry,
orange and lime. Serve immediately.

GiN SWiZZLE

SERVES 1

INGREDIENTS

100 g/3½ oz whisky-barrel woodchips

350 ml/12 fl oz gin

1 measure lime juice

2 tsp caster sugar

1 tsp Angostura bitters

large handful of crushed ice

175 ml/6 fl oz soda water

lime slice, to decorate

FACT

The swizzle originates from the West Indies, sometime around the early 1900s. This version is made with whiskey-barrel smoked gin.

1.
This cocktail takes 2 weeks to infuse and you will need a blowtorch. Lay the woodchips on a metal tray and place onto a heatproof surface.

2.
Using a blowtorch, scorch all over the woodchips until about half have blackened. Put the scorched woodchips into a sterilized, sealable jar, then pour in the gin. Keep the gin bottle for later use. Mix and seal the jar. Leave in a cool place for 2 weeks.

3.
Strain the gin through a fine sieve. Place 2 measures of smoked gin, the lime juice, caster sugar and bitters into a highball glass. The rest of the gin can be stored for up to 2 months. Add the ice to the glass and top up with the soda water. Froth well with a swizzle stick and serve immediately with a lime slice.

Shaking & Stirring

TOM COLLINS

SERVES 1

1.
Put the cracked ice cubes into a cocktail shaker.

2.
Pour over the gin, lemon juice and sugar syrup and shake vigorously until well frosted.

3.
Strain the cocktail into a chilled Collins or highball glass.

4.
Top up with soda water and decorate with the lemon slice. Serve immediately.

INGREDIENTS

4–6 cracked ice cubes

3 measures gin

2 measures lemon juice

½ measure sugar syrup

soda water

lemon slice, to decorate

BLACK RUSSIAN

SERVES 1

1.
Pour the vodka and coffee liqueur over cracked ice cubes into a chilled lowball glass.

2.
Stir well with a bar spoon to mix.

3.
Serve immediately.

INGREDIENTS

2 measures vodka

1 measure coffee liqueur

cracked ice cubes

Shaking & Stirring

CUBA LIBRE

SERVES 1

1.
Half-fill a highball glass with cracked ice.

2.
Pour over the rum.

3.
Top up with cola.

4.
Stir gently to mix and decorate with the lime wedge. Serve immediately.

INGREDIENTS

cracked ice cubes

2 measures white rum

cola

lime wedge, to decorate

BVD

SERVES 1

1.
Pour the brandy, dry vermouth and Dubonnet over cracked ice in a mixing glass.

2.
Stir to mix and strain into a chilled coupe glass. Serve immediately.

INGREDIENTS

1 measure brandy

1 measure dry vermouth

1 measure Dubonnet

cracked ice cubes

GINGER WHISKY MAC

SERVES 1

1.
Pour the whisky into a lowball glass.

2.
Add the ginger wine.

3.
Add a few ice cubes and lightly stir.

4.
Serve immediately.

INGREDIENTS

2 measures Scotch whisky

1 measure ginger wine

whole ice cubes

DAIQUIRI

SERVES 1

1.
Put the cracked ice cubes into a cocktail shaker.

2.
Pour the rum, lime juice and sugar syrup over the ice cubes.

3.
Shake vigorously until well frosted.

4.
Strain into a chilled martini glass and decorate with a wedge of lime. Serve immediately.

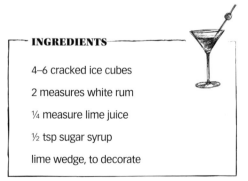

INGREDIENTS

4–6 cracked ice cubes

2 measures white rum

¼ measure lime juice

½ tsp sugar syrup

lime wedge, to decorate

Shaking & Stirring

COSMOPOLITAN

1.
Put the cracked ice cubes into a cocktail shaker.

2.
Pour the liquid ingredients over the ice cubes.

3.
Shake vigorously until well frosted.

4.
Strain into a chilled martini glass and decorate with the orange peel. Serve immediately.

INGREDIENTS

4–6 cracked ice cubes

2 measures vodka

1 measure triple sec

1 measure lime juice

1 measure cranberry juice

orange peel strip, to decorate

VIRGIN COLLINS

SERVES 1

1.
Put the mint leaves into a chilled Collins or highball glass.

2.
Add the sugar and lemon juice.

3.
Crush the mint leaves, then stir until the sugar has dissolved.

4.
Fill the glass with cracked ice cubes and top up with sparkling water. Stir gently and decorate with the fresh mint and lemon slice. Serve immediately.

INGREDIENTS

6 fresh mint leaves, plus extra to decorate

1 tsp caster sugar

2 measures lemon juice

cracked ice cubes

sparkling water

lemon slice, to decorate

77

Shaking & Stirring

EL DIABLO

SERVES 1

1.
Add the tequila, lime juice and cassis to a cocktail shaker filled with ice.

2.
Shake vigorously until well frosted. Strain into a chilled highball glass filled with ice.

3.
Top up with ginger ale. Decorate the glass with the lime slice. Serve immediately.

INGREDIENTS

1 measure tequila

½ measure lime juice

½ measure crème de cassis

cracked ice cubes

ginger ale

lime slice, to decorate

SIDECAR

1.
Put the cracked ice cubes into a cocktail shaker. Pour the liquid ingredients over the ice cubes.

2.
Shake vigorously until well frosted.

3.
Strain into a chilled martini glass and decorate with the orange peel. Serve immediately.

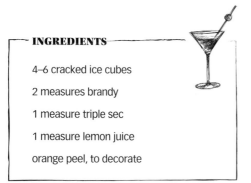

INGREDIENTS

4–6 cracked ice cubes

2 measures brandy

1 measure triple sec

1 measure lemon juice

orange peel, to decorate

THE HISTORY OF THE SHRUB

The shrub cocktail has revived in popularity over the last few years, partly because of an increased interest in fermented flavours and also because of the rise of crafted, botanical cocktails. Shrubs are traditionally made with fruit, sugar and vinegar to create a sharp yet sweet concoction and can be made with a large variety of spirits, including whiskey, rum, vodka, brandy, sherry or gin. The shrub is a classic cocktail dating back to the 1700s and its name is derived from an Arabic word meaning 'to drink'. Shrubs were commonly drunk in both the UK and the USA throughout the 18th and 19th centuries and even continued to enjoy popularity during America's Prohibition era as it was a tasty, thirst-quenching beverage even without the alcohol. It faded into partial obscurity after the 1930s but shrubs are now on trend again and are often served as an aperitif because of their slight acidity. There are two flavour-packed shrub cocktails on pages 82–85.

GOOSEBERRY SHRUB

SERVES 1

INGREDIENTS

200 g/7 oz gooseberries

400 g/14 oz caster sugar

500 ml/18 fl oz raw cider vinegar

whole ice cubes

2 measures bourbon

1 tsp Angostura bitters

orange wedge, to decorate

FACT

A gooseberry may be green, white, yellow or have shades ranging from pink to deep purple. The European gooseberry can grow as large as a small plum, but tends to be around 2½ cm/1 inch long.

1.
This cocktail takes 2 days to infuse. In a mixing bowl, muddle the gooseberries and sugar until the gooseberries have broken down. Cover and leave in the refrigerator to macerate for 24 hours. Remove from the refrigerator and mix in the vinegar. Cover and leave in the refrigerator for another 24 hours.

2.
Strain the liquid through muslin, discarding the solids. Pour the liquid into a sterilized, sealable jar.

3.
Pour 2 measures of the gooseberry syrup into an ice-filled lowball glass. Add the bourbon and bitters and stir. Any remaining syrup can be stored in the refrigerator for up to 2 months.

4.
Decorate with the orange wedge and serve immediately.

POMEGRANATE & MINT SHRUB

SERVES 1

INGREDIENTS

200 g/7 oz pomegranate seeds

400 g/14 oz caster sugar

20 mint leaves

500 ml/18 fl oz raw cider vinegar

crushed ice

1 measure gin

1 measure Grand Marnier

sprig of mint, to decorate

1 tsp pomegranate seeds, to decorate

TIP
Try making variations with other fruits, such as raspberries, blackberries, strawberries, blueberries and redcurrants.

1.
This cocktail takes 2 days to infuse. In a medium bowl, muddle the pomegranate seeds, sugar and mint until the seeds are crushed. Cover and leave in the refrigerator to macerate for 24 hours. Remove from the refrigerator and stir in the vinegar. Cover again and leave for another 24 hours.

2.
Strain the mixture through a muslin. Pour into a sterilized, sealable jar.

3.
Fill a highball glass with crushed ice. Add 2 measures of the pomegranate syrup to the glass. The rest of the pomegranate syrup can be stored in the refrigerator for up to 2 months.

4.
Add the gin and Grand Marnier to the glass and stir with a bar spoon. Decorate with the mint and pomegranate and serve immediately.

CRANBERRY COLLINS

SERVES 1

1.
Put 4–6 cracked ice cubes into a cocktail shaker.

2.
Pour over the vodka, elderflower cordial and cranberry juice and shake until well frosted.

3.
Strain into a Collins or highball glass filled with cracked ice. Top up with soda water and decorate with the lime slice and peel. Serve immediately.

INGREDIENTS

cracked ice cubes

2 measures vodka

¾ measure elderflower cordial

3 measures cranberry juice

soda water

lime slice and lime peel twist, to decorate

KLONDIKE COOLER

1.
Put the sugar into a chilled lowball glass and add the ginger ale. Stir until all the sugar has dissolved.

2.
Fill the glass with cracked ice. Pour over the whiskey.

3.
Top up with the sparkling water. Stir gently and decorate with the lemon peel twist. Serve immediately.

INGREDIENTS

½ tsp icing sugar

1 measure ginger ale

cracked ice cubes

2 measures blended whiskey

sparkling water

lemon peel twist, to decorate

KIMCHI & WASABI BLOODY MARY

SERVES 1

INGREDIENTS

1 measure vodka

1 measure sake

½ measure lime juice

½ tsp Korean chilli powder

¼ tsp garlic granules

2.5-cm/1-inch piece fresh ginger, grated

1 tsp fish sauce

½ tsp wasabi paste

2 tsp tonkatsu bulldog sauce or other hot sauce

whole ice cubes

175 ml/6 fl oz tomato juice

mooli radish stick, to decorate

TIP

This is great served with oysters and you can adjust the seasonings to taste.

1.
Mix together the vodka, sake, lime juice, chilli powder, garlic granules, ginger, fish sauce, wasabi paste and bulldog sauce in a Collins or highball glass, using a bar spoon.

2.
Stir well, making sure all the ingredients are well combined.

3.
Add a few ice cubes and the tomato juice and stir again.

4.
Decorate with the mooli radish and serve immediately.

BUILDING & LAYERING

Building is a mixology technique, a technical term for the task of pouring all the ingredients, one by one, usually over ice, into the glass in which the cocktail will be served. You might then stir the cocktail briefly, but this is just to mix rather than for chilling or aerating. It is important to follow built recipes exactly as the order of the ingredients can change from drink to drink and this can affect the final flavour.

Another important skill that the bartender must acquire is the art of layering, which requires greater concentration, precision and a steadier hand. To make layered shooters or other drinks, you generally pour the heaviest liquid first, working through to the lightest. However, the real trick is the technique. Either touch the top of the drink with a long-handled bar spoon and pour the liquid slowly over the back of it to disperse it across the top of the ingredients already in the glass, or pour the liquid down the twisted stem that many bar spoons have. You should hold the spoon's flat disc just above the drink. Be sure to use a clean bar spoon for each layer. Floating is the term used to describe adding the top layer.

Building & Layering

VODKA ESPRESSO

SERVES 1

1.
Put the cracked ice into a cocktail shaker.

2.
Pour in the coffee and vodka, add the sugar and shake vigorously until well frosted.

3.
Strain into a chilled martini glass.

4.
Float the liqueur on top by pouring the Amarula over the back of a teaspoon or bar spoon over the top of the coffee mixture in the glass.

5.
Decorate with coffee beans, if using, and serve immediately.

INGREDIENTS

4–6 cracked ice cubes

2 measures cooled espresso, plus beans to decorate (optional)

1 measure vodka

2 tsp caster sugar

1 measure Amarula

Building & Layering

94

ELDERFLOWER CHAMPAGNE FIZZ

SERVES 1

INGREDIENTS

1.5 kg/3 lb 5 oz caster sugar

1 litre/1¾ pints water

1 lemon, sliced

15 elderflower heads, washed

40 g/1½ oz citric acid, available from chemists or hardware stores

½ measure vodka

150 ml/5 fl oz chilled champagne

1.
This cocktail takes 24 hours to infuse. In a medium saucepan, bring the sugar and water to a gentle simmer. Turn off the heat and add the lemon slices, elderflower heads and citric acid. Cover the pan and leave to infuse for 24 hours.

2.
Strain the syrup through a sieve. Then strain again through a muslin to catch all the small bits.

3.
Pour into sterilized, sealable jars. This will keep for several months in a cool place.

4.
Pour ½ measure of the elderflower syrup into a champagne flute. Add the vodka and then top up with the champagne.

5.
Serve immediately.

Building & Layering

VIRGIN GINGER FIZZ

SERVES 1

1.
Put 2 measures of ginger ale into a blender.

2.
Add the mint sprigs and blend together.

3.
Strain into a chilled highball glass that is two-thirds filled with cracked ice. Top up with more ginger ale.

4.
Decorate with raspberries and the mint sprig. Serve immediately.

INGREDIENTS

ginger ale

3 fresh mint sprigs

cracked ice cubes

fresh raspberries and
a sprig of mint, to decorate

LAYERED ESPRESSO SHOT

SERVES 1

1.
Pour the Galliano into a shot glass.

2.
With a steady hand, carefully pour in the espresso over the back of a teaspoon or bar spoon that is held against the inside of the glass, to make a second layer.

3.
Carefully pour in the double cream in the same way, to create a third top layer.

4.
Serve immediately.

INGREDIENTS

¾ measure Galliano

¾ measure hot espresso

½ measure double cream

AURORA BOREALIS

1.
Pour the grappa slowly over the back of a spoon around one side of a well chilled shot glass.

2.
Gently pour the Chartreuse around the other side.

3.
Pour the curaçao gently into the middle.

4.
Add the drops of crème de cassis. Serve immediately.

INGREDIENTS

1 measure chilled grappa or vodka

1 measure chilled green Chartreuse

½ measure chilled orange curaçao

3 drops chilled crème de cassis

Building & Layering 98

BELLINI

SERVES 1

1.
Rub the rim of a chilled champagne flute with the lemon wedge.

2.
Put the sugar in a saucer, then dip the rim of the flute in it.

3.
Pour the peach juice into the flute.

4.
Top up with the champagne.
Serve immediately.

INGREDIENTS

1 lemon wedge

caster sugar

1 measure peach juice

3 measures chilled champagne

NEGRONI

SERVES 1

1.
Place the cracked ice cubes into a mixing glass.

2.
Pour the gin, Campari and vermouth over the ice.

3.
Strain into a lowball glass and decorate with the orange twist. Serve immediately.

INGREDIENTS

6 cracked ice cubes

1 measure gin

1 measure Campari

½ measure sweet vermouth

twist of orange peel, to decorate

HOT BUTTERED RUM

SERVES 1

1.
In a lowball glass, mix together the rum, brown sugar and hot water with a teaspoon until the sugar has completely dissolved.

2.
Place the butter on top.

3.
Sprinkle over the allspice.

4.
When the butter has melted, serve immediately.

INGREDIENTS

1 measure dark rum

1 tsp soft dark brown sugar

150 ml/5 fl oz hot water

1 tsp salted butter

¼ tsp allspice

Building & Layering

WHISKEY SANGAREE

SERVES 1

1.
Put the ice in a chilled lowball glass.

2.
Pour over the bourbon and sugar syrup.

3.
Top up with soda water.

4.
Stir gently to mix, then pour the port over the top. Sprinkle over the grated nutmeg. Serve immediately.

INGREDIENTS

4–6 whole ice cubes

2 measures bourbon

1 tsp sugar syrup

soda water

1 tbsp ruby port

¼ tsp grated nutmeg, to decorate

B-52

INGREDIENTS

1 measure chilled dark crème de cacao

1 measure chilled Irish cream

1 measure chilled Grand Marnier

1.
Pour the crème de cacao into a shot glass.

2.
With a steady hand, gently pour in the Irish cream over the back of a teaspoon or bar spoon to make a second layer.

3.
Gently pour in the Grand Marnier over the back of a teaspoon or bar spoon.

4.
Serve with layers intact or cover with your hand and slam to mix. Serve immediately.

Building & Layering

A SLOE KISS

INGREDIENTS

4–6 cracked ice cubes

½ measure sloe gin

½ measure Southern Comfort

1 measure vodka

1 tsp amaretto

1 tsp Galliano

orange juice

orange peel twist, to decorate

1.
Put the cracked ice cubes into a cocktail shaker. Pour over the sloe gin, Southern Comfort, vodka and amaretto and shake vigorously until well frosted.

2.
Strain into a long, chilled highball glass filled with cracked ice.

3.
Splash on the Galliano.

4.
Top up with orange juice and decorate with the orange peel. Serve immediately.

Building & Layering

KIR ROYALE

SERVES 1

1.
Put the cassis into the bottom of a champagne flute.

2.
Add the brandy.

3.
Top up with champagne.

4.
Decorate with the mint sprig. Serve immediately.

INGREDIENTS

3 drops crème de cassis, or to taste

½ measure brandy

champagne, chilled

fresh mint sprig, to decorate

MOLECULAR COCKTAILS

Molecular mixology originates from the world of experimental gastronomy where chefs first used molecular techniques in their food recipes. This trend soon caught on and mixologists started using these same methods in their bartending. Molecular mixology is where science combines with cocktails to create some incredible results – from dry ice effects to drinks with overflowing bubbles or frozen nitro cocktails. Other popular molecular techniques include drinks topped with candyfloss, cocktails that have ingredients suspended in the drink, hot infused drinks, cocktails that change colour, and cocktail jellies, ice pops or marshmallows.

A lot of molecular cocktails created in bars are made with expensive and elaborate equipment but some of the more simple techniques can be done in the home. Foams and airs can be made in any kitchen using some basic equipment and they add an attractive finish to most cocktails (see page 13 for some basic foam and air recipes and page 108 for a foam-topped cocktail). Dry ice can used to produce a dramatic effect and creates an impressive entrance when serving up a tray of drinks to friends – a punch served with dry ice can be found on page 110.

MESCAL & WATERMELON FOAM

INGREDIENTS

1 egg white

½ measure lemon juice

1 tsp caster sugar

2 measures mescal

1 measure triple sec

2 measures watermelon juice

whole ice cubes

TIP

Foams work well with any fruit-based or sour cocktails.

1.
To make the foam, you need an espuma gun. In a bowl, lightly whisk the egg white, lemon juice and sugar until the sugar has dissolved. Pour into an espuma gun and charge once.

2.
Place the mescal, triple sec and watermelon juice into an ice-filled cocktail shaker.

3.
Shake vigorously until well frosted. Strain the cocktail into two coupe or coupette glasses.

4.
Shake the espuma gun and then top the cocktails with the egg white foam.

5.
Serve immediately.

DRY-ICE PUNCH

SERVES 8

INGREDIENTS

150 ml/5 fl oz bourbon, chilled

150 ml/5 fl oz limoncello, chilled

150 ml/5 fl oz amaretto, chilled

2 measures grenadine

500 ml/18 fl oz cloudy apple juice, chilled

500 ml/18 fl oz orange juice, chilled

2 oranges, sliced

2 apples, sliced

100 g/3½ oz dry ice pellets (optional)

WARNING
Dry ice is a hazardous substance and can cause severe burns if it comes into contact with skin and eyes. Do not leave dry ice unattended around children. Ensure protective gloves, such as oven gloves, are worn at all times when handling the ice, as well as any tools or containers in contact with it. Do not store dry ice in an airtight container and always use in a well-ventilated area. Always read the instructions supplied with dry ice.

1.
Arrange to have the dry ice delivered on the day of use as it has a very short shelf life. You will also need gloves and a scoop.

2.
Pour the bourbon, limoncello, amaretto, grenadine, apple and orange juice into a large punch bowl. Add the orange and apple slices.

3.
Place the punch bowl in a large, deep tray, filled with water.

4.
If creating the dry ice, use gloves and a scoop to tip the pellets evenly into the water. The punch is ready to serve immediately. The foggy effect will only last for about 5 minutes. Once it has cleared, simply add some more dry ice in the same way.

Building & Layering

TRICOLOUR

1.
Pour the maraschino into a chilled shot glass.

2.
Gently pour in the crème de menthe over the back of a teaspoon or bar spoon to make a second layer.

3.
Gently pour in the Irish cream over the back of a teaspoon or bar spoon.

4.
Decorate with the mint leaf and serve immediately.

INGREDIENTS

1 measure chilled red maraschino liqueur

1 measure chilled crème de menthe

1 measure chilled Irish cream

fresh mint leaf, to decorate

RATTLESNAKE

SERVES 1

INGREDIENTS

1 measure chilled dark crème de cacao

1 measure chilled Irish cream

1 measure chilled Kahlúa

cocktail cherry, to decorate

1.
Pour the crème de cacao into a shot glass.

2.
With a steady hand, gently pour in the Irish cream over the back of a teaspoon or bar spoon to make a second layer.

3.
Pour in the Kahlúa over the back of a teaspoon or bar spoon to make a third layer.

4.
Decorate with the cherry and serve immediately.

Building & Layering

AMARETTO, IRISH CREAM & BOURBON

SERVES 1

1.
Gently pour the amaretto into a shot glass.

2.
With a steady hand, carefully pour in the Irish cream over the back of a teaspoon or bar spoon to make a second layer.

3.
Carefully pour in the bourbon in the same way, to create a third top layer.

4.
Serve immediately.

INGREDIENTS

½ measure amaretto

½ measure Irish cream

½ measure bourbon

THE BENTLEY

SERVES 1

1.
Mix the cognac, peach brandy and passion fruit juice gently together in a chilled mixing glass.

2.
Pour the mixture into a coupe or coupette glass. Add one ice cube and slowly pour in champagne.

3.
Serve immediately.

INGREDIENTS

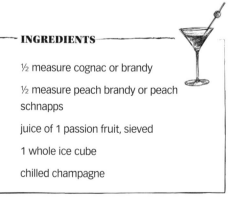

½ measure cognac or brandy

½ measure peach brandy or peach schnapps

juice of 1 passion fruit, sieved

1 whole ice cube

chilled champagne

CIDER BREEZE

SERVES 1

1.
Add the rum to a chilled highball glass that is half-filled with ice cubes.

2.
Top up with the cider.

3.
Decorate the glass with the apple slice and serve immediately.

INGREDIENTS

1 measure coconut rum

whole ice cubes

sparkling cider

apple slice, to decorate

PINK HEATHER

1.
Pour the whisky and the strawberry liqueur into a chilled champagne flute.

2.
Top up the flute with chilled sparkling wine and decorate the rim of the glass with a strawberry.

3.
Serve immediately.

INGREDIENTS

1 measure Scotch whisky

1 measure strawberry liqueur

chilled sparkling wine

fresh strawberry, to decorate

SAZERAC

SERVES 1

INGREDIENTS

1 tsp absinthe

1 large ice cube

½ measure sugar syrup

3 tsp Angostura bitters

3 tsp Peychaud's aromatic bitters

2 measures rye whiskey

lemon zest, to decorate

FACT

The Sazerac is now made with rye whiskey, following the destruction of European vineyards in the 19th century, which created a shortage of the Sazarac cognac that gave the cocktail its name.

1.
Swill the absinthe around the inside of a lowball glass.

2.
Add the ice cube, then the sugar syrup and then both of the bitters and the rye whiskey.

3.
Rub the lemon zest around the rim of the glass.

4.
Serve immediately, with the lemon zest in the glass.

MUDDLING
&
BLENDING

MUDDLING & BLENDING

Muddling is the term used to describe the extraction of the juice or oils from the pulp or skin of a fruit, herb or spice. It involves mashing ingredients to release their flavours and it's usually done with a wooden pestle-like implement called a muddler. The end that is used to crush ingredients is thicker and rounded and the opposite, thinner end is used to stir. The best muddling technique is to keep pressing down with a twisting action until the ingredient has released all of its oil or juice. If you don't have a muddler, you can use a pestle and mortar or the end of a wooden spoon. The most well-known muddled drinks are the Mojito and the Caipirinha.

As the name suggests, blending is when all the ingredients are combined together in a blender or food processor. This technique is often used when mixing alcohol with fruit or with creamy ingredients that do not combine well unless they are blended. These drinks are often blended with crushed or cracked ice to produce cocktails with a smooth, frozen consistency. Popular blended drinks are Frozen Daiquiris and Coladas.

LIME & LEMON GRASS SLING

SERVES 1

INGREDIENTS

½ lime

1 small lemon grass stick, trimmed

2 measures gin

½ measure Benedictine

½ measure cherry brandy liqueur

2 dashes orange bitters

whole ice cubes

150 ml/5 fl oz soda water

lemon slice and fresh cherry,
to decorate

TIP
This recipe is slightly on the dry side
of a traditional sling. If you have a
slightly sweeter tooth, substitute the
soda water with pineapple juice.

1.
Cut the lime into wedges and then
slice the lemon grass thinly.

2.
Place the lime and lemon grass into a
cocktail shaker.

3.
Using a muddler, crush the lime and
the lemon grass to release the juice
and oils.

4.
Add the gin, Benedictine, cherry
brandy and orange bitters to the
cocktail shaker.

5.
Pour the mixture into a sling or
highball glass. Add some ice cubes
and top up with soda water. Decorate
with the lemon slice and cherry and
serve immediately.

BEER & RUM FLIP

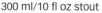

INGREDIENTS

300 ml/10 fl oz stout

2 measures dark rum

2 measures maple syrup

2 eggs

½ tsp nutmeg, to decorate

TIP

This is a warming drink for a winter's night or to celebrate St Patrick's Day with a bang!

1.
Gently heat the stout in a medium saucepan over a medium heat.

2.
Pour the rum and maple syrup into a blender. Crack in the eggs.

3.
When the stout has almost come to the boil, pour it carefully into the blender and blend for 30 seconds, or until the contents are nice and frothy.

4.
Divide the flip between four snifter glasses and decorate each drink with a little nutmeg.

5.
Serve immediately.

RUM COOLER

SERVES 1

1.
Put 2–4 cracked ice cubes, the rum, pineapple juice and banana into a blender.

2.
Add the lime juice and blend for about 1 minute or until smooth.

3.
Fill a chilled lowball glass with cracked ice and pour over the cocktail.

4.
Decorate with the lime peel. Serve immediately.

INGREDIENTS

cracked ice cubes

1½ measures white rum

1½ measures pineapple juice

1 banana, peeled and sliced

juice of 1 lime

lime peel twist, to decorate

WHITE RUSSIAN BLENDED SHAKE

SERVES 4

1.
Place all of the ingredients into a blender and blend thoroughly until smooth.

2.
Divide between four lowball glasses.

3.
Sprinkle each glass with some of the salt.

4.
Serve immediately with a straw.

┌─ **INGREDIENTS** ─────────────

4 measures vodka

4 measures Kahlúa

4 scoops vanilla ice cream

handful of whole ice cubes

½ tsp sea salt crystals

MOJITO

1.
Put the sugar syrup, mint leaves and lime juice into a lowball glass.

2.
Muddle the mint leaves, then add the cracked ice cubes and the rum.

3.
Top up with soda water.

4.
Finish with the Angostura bitters and decorate with the remaining mint leaves. Serve immediately.

INGREDIENTS

1 tsp sugar syrup

6 fresh mint leaves, plus extra to decorate

juice of ½ lime

4–6 cracked ice cubes

2 measures Jamaican rum

soda water

1 tsp Angostura bitters

Muddling & Blending

CAIPIRINHA

SERVES 1

1.
Put the lime wedges into a chilled lowball glass.

2.
Add the sugar to the lowball glass.

3.
Muddle the lime wedges, then pour the cachaça into the glass.

4.
Fill the glass with the cracked ice and stir well. Serve immediately.

INGREDIENTS

6 lime wedges

2 tsp granulated sugar

3 measures cachaça

4–6 cracked ice cubes

PIÑA COLADA

SERVES 1

1.
Put the crushed ice cubes in a blender.
Pour over the white rum, dark rum and
pineapple juice.

2.
Add the coconut cream to the blender and
blend until smooth.

3.
Pour, without straining, into a chilled
goblet or wine glass.

4.
Decorate with the cocktail cherry and the
pineapple wedge. Serve immediately.

INGREDIENTS

4–6 crushed ice cubes

2 measures white rum

1 measure dark rum

3 measures pineapple juice

2 measures coconut cream

cocktail cherry and pineapple wedge,
to decorate

MANDARIN & LIME GINGER BEER

SERVES 1

INGREDIENTS

1 lime

½ mandarin

2 measures dark rum

whole ice cubes

150 ml/5 fl oz ginger beer

lime wedges, to decorate

1.
Cut the lime and mandarin into wedges.

2.
Place the lime and mandarin into a cocktail shaker. Use a muddler for about 10 seconds to crush the fruit and to release its oils.

3.
Add the rum and stir with a bar spoon.

4.
Pour the rum mixture into a Collins or highball glass.

5.
Add a few ice cubes and top up with the ginger beer.

6.
Decorate with lime wedges and serve immediately with a straw.

MIDNIGHT COWBOY

SERVES 1

1.
Slowly blend together the brandy, coffee liqueur, cream and crushed ice in a blender until frothy.

2.
Pour into a chilled martini glass. Top up with cola and serve immediately.

INGREDIENTS

1 measure brandy

½ measure coffee liqueur

½ measure single cream, chilled

crushed ice

cola

DIRTY MONKEY HARD SHAKE

SERVES 1

1.
Place the vodka, chocolate syrup, banana, coconut milk and ice cubes into a blender or food processor.

2.
Blend the mixture for about 1 minute, or until completely smooth.

3.
Pour into a chilled Collins or highball glass.

4.
Decorate with the grated chocolate and serve immediately.

INGREDIENTS

2 measures vodka

2 measures chocolate syrup

1 banana, peeled and chopped

2 measures coconut milk

handful of whole ice cubes

5 g/⅛ oz grated plain chocolate, to decorate

BELLE COLLINS

SERVES 1

INGREDIENTS

2 fresh mint sprigs,
plus extra to decorate

2 measures gin

1 measure lemon juice

1 tsp sugar syrup

4–6 crushed ice cubes

sparkling water

1.
Muddle the mint sprigs in a mixing glass.

2.
Place the mint in a chilled lowball glass and pour in the gin, lemon juice and sugar syrup.

3.
Add the crushed ice cubes to the glass.

4.
Top up with sparkling water, stir gently and decorate with more fresh mint. Serve immediately.

MINT JULEP

SERVES 1

1.
Strip the leaves from the mint sprig and put in a chilled lowball glass.

2.
Crush the mint leaves and pour in the sugar syrup.

3.
Half-fill the glass with cracked ice and stir.

4.
Add the bourbon and decorate with a mint sprig. Serve immediately.

INGREDIENTS

1 fresh mint sprig, plus extra to decorate

1 tbsp sugar syrup

cracked ice cubes

3 measures bourbon

Muddling & Blending

CRAFT INGREDIENTS

Craft cocktails have introduced a whole new range of ingredients into the world of mixology and cocktail menus now feature a huge array of interesting and unusual flavours. Fresh herbs are frequently used in contemporary cocktail making, particularly strong flavours such as basil, rosemary, thyme and mint. Other more unusual fresh ingredients include lavender, elderflower and rose petals, which each add a floral and slightly sweet taste to drinks. Other sweeteners that are used in craft cocktails as alternatives to processed sugars are honey, agave syrup and maple syrup, which provide a more natural sweetness.

Artisan mixologists also like to infuse other types of drinks into cocktails to create some interesting cocktail hybrids. Tea flavours are very popular to use in craft cocktails, from the simple breakfast tea through to more specialist blends such as Earl Grey, green tea and smoky lapsang souchong. Beer cocktails are also becoming more common, using craft ale or stouts mixed with spirits and other ingredients to create some strong but flavourful combinations. Cider cocktails are also rising in popularity due to the resurgence of craft ciders, scrumpies and perries.

PEACH ICE TEA

SERVES 4

INGREDIENTS

2 overripe peaches

1 measure tequila

1 measure gin

1 measure Bacardi

1 measure triple sec

1 measure vodka

1 measure lemon juice

1 measure lime juice

1 measure sugar syrup

2 large handfuls of crushed ice

660 ml/1 pint 2 fl oz cola

fresh peach slices, to decorate

1.
Cut the peaches in half, remove the stones and peel away the skin.

2.
Place all the ingredients, except the cola, into a blender and blend until you have a slushie consistency.

3.
Divide the mixture between four sling or hurricane glasses.

4.
Top up with cola and decorate the glasses with fresh peach slices.

5.
Serve immediately.

TIP
You could also use other soft fruits instead of peaches, such as apricots, cherries, plums or even pineapple.

BLOODHOUND

SERVES 1

1.
Put the gin, sweet vermouth, dry vermouth and 3 strawberries into a blender.

2.
Add the cracked ice.

3.
Blend until smooth.

4.
Pour into a chilled martini glass and decorate with the remaining strawberry. Serve immediately.

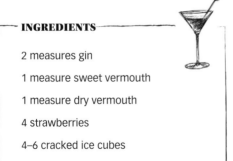

INGREDIENTS

2 measures gin

1 measure sweet vermouth

1 measure dry vermouth

4 strawberries

4–6 cracked ice cubes

FROZEN PEACH DAIQUIRI

SERVES 1

1.
Put the crushed ice and the peach into a blender.

2.
Add the rum, lime juice and sugar syrup and blend to a slushie consistency.

3.
Pour into a chilled martini glass.

4.
Decorate with the peach slice and serve immediately.

INGREDIENTS

4–6 crushed ice cubes

½ peach, stoned and chopped

2 measures white rum

1 measure lime juice

1 tsp sugar syrup

peach slice, to decorate

Muddling & Blending

VIRGIN RASPBERRY COOLERS

SERVES 4

1.
Cut the ends off the lemons, then scoop out and chop the flesh.

2.
Put the lemon flesh in a blender with the sugar, raspberries, vanilla extract and 4–6 cracked ice cubes and blend for 2–3 minutes.

3.
Half-fill four highball glasses with cracked ice and strain in the lemon mixture.

4.
Top up with sparkling water and decorate with the mint sprigs. Serve immediately.

INGREDIENTS

2 lemons

115 g/4 oz icing sugar

115 g/4 oz raspberries

4 drops vanilla extract

cracked ice cubes

sparkling water

fresh mint sprigs, to decorate

Muddling & Blending   144

STRAWBERRY COLADA

SERVES 1

1.
Put the crushed ice in a blender.

2.
Add the rum, pineapple juice and coconut cream.

3.
Add the strawberries to the blender. Blend until smooth.

4.
Pour, without straining, into a chilled highball glass. Decorate with the pineapple wedge and strawberry half. Serve immediately.

┌─ **INGREDIENTS** ─

4–6 crushed ice cubes

3 measures golden rum

4 measures pineapple juice

1 measure coconut cream

6 strawberries

pineapple wedge and halved strawberry, to decorate

FLIRTINI

SERVES 1

1.
Put the pineapple into a mixing glass or jug.

2.
Crush the pineapple and add the orange liqueur, vodka and pineapple juice. Stir well.

3.
Strain into a wine or lowball glass.

4.
Top up with the champagne and serve immediately.

INGREDIENTS

¼ slice fresh pineapple, chopped

½ measure chilled orange liqueur

½ measure chilled vodka

1 measure chilled pineapple juice

champagne, chilled

PLACEMAKER PUNCH

SERVES 4

1.
Place the fruit and sugar into a large punch bowl.

2.
Add a little water and crush together using a muddler.

3.
Add the maraschino and sparkling water and mix well.

4.
Top up with the champagne. Decorate with the mint leaves and strawberry slices. Serve immediately.

INGREDIENTS

25 strawberries

½ small fresh pineapple, peeled and finely chopped

1–2 tbsp icing sugar

1 measure maraschino liqueur

225 ml/8 fl oz sparkling water

1 bottle dry champagne

fresh mint leaves and sliced strawberries, to decorate

Muddling & Blending

GRAPEFRUIT & CHERRY GIN & TONIC

SERVES 1

INGREDIENTS

1 slice of grapefruit

4 cherries, stoned

2 measures gin

whole ice cubes

175 ml/6 fl oz tonic water

2 cherries, to decorate

TIP
This would also work with any other citrus fruit, such as oranges, and any other soft fruit, such as blueberries.

1.
Cut the grapefruit slice into chunks.

2.
Place the grapefruit and cherries into a cocktail shaker.

3.
Using a muddler, crush the grapefruit and cherries for about 30 seconds to release the flavour and oils.

4.
Add the gin to the cocktail shaker and stir. Pour the mixture into a Collins or highball glass.

5.
Add some ice cubes to the glass and top up with tonic water.

6.
Decorate with cherries on top and serve immediately.

MOJITO ICE POPS

MAKES 8 ICE POPS

INGREDIENTS

juice of 6 limes

600 ml/1 pint chilled soda water

50 g/1¾ oz fresh mint leaves

3 limes, cut into wedges

100 g/3½ oz caster sugar

2 tbsp white rum

1.
Put the lime juice and soda water into a measuring jug and stir together well.

2.
Stir in the mint leaves, lime wedges, sugar and rum. Using a muddler, mash together all the ingredients until well blended.

3.
Pour the mixture into 8 x 100 ml/3½ fl oz ice pop moulds. Divide the lime wedges and mint leaves evenly between them. Insert eight ice pop sticks and freeze for 10–12 hours, or until firm.

4.
To unmould the ice pops, dip the frozen moulds into warm water for a few seconds and gently release the pops while holding the sticks.

Muddling & Blending   **150**

BLACK RUSSIAN ICE POPS

MAKES 8 ICE POPS

1.

Put all the ingredients into a measuring jug and stir together well.

2.

Pour the mixture into 8 x 50 ml/2 fl oz ice pop moulds or thick shot glasses. Insert eight ice pop sticks and freeze for 8–10 hours, or until firm.

3.

To unmould the ice pops, wrap the frozen moulds or glasses in a hot water-soaked tea-towel for a few seconds and gently release the pops while holding the sticks.

INGREDIENTS

1 tbsp Kahlúa or Tia Maria

500 ml/18 fl oz cola

2 tbsp vodka

BLACKBERRY MARGARITA

INGREDIENTS

200 g/7 oz blackberries

handful of whole ice cubes

1 tbsp caster sugar

8 measures tequila

4 measures triple sec

2 measures lime juice

1 lime wedge

1 tbsp sea salt

4 blackberries, to decorate

4 mint sprigs, to decorate

TIP
This would make a great drink to start or end an evening as it has a clean, refreshing taste.

1.
Place the blackberries, ice cubes, caster sugar, tequila, triple sec and lime juice into a blender.

2.
Blend the mixture for about 1 minute, or until completely smooth.

3.
Rub the rims of four chilled margarita glasses with the lime wedge. Place the sea salt on a small plate and roll the rims in the salt.

4.
Divide the cocktail carefully between the four glasses.

5.
Decorate with the blackberries and mint and serve immediately.

BITTERS & SOURS

BITTERS & SOURS

Using bitters in mixology is a complex process – too much and the drink becomes unpleasant to the taste buds, but the right combination of bitterness with sweetness can produce some tasty, refreshing cocktails. Adding bitters lightly in drops or dashes can help create a slightly moreish taste, and some sweetness or a pinch or two of salt can help reduce the effect of the bitterness. Some common bitters that can be used in mixology are tonic water, bitter lemon and Angostura bitters, as well as other types of bitters, such as Campari and orange bitters.

Sours were first made in the American South in the mid-19th century. They were originally made with brandy before American whiskey replaced it as the main spirit of choice, although sours are now often made with gin or vodka too. Whatever the spirit, the key ingredient of a sour is citrus juice along with a sweetener, such as triple sec, fruit juice or sugar syrup. Sours are usually mixed by being shaken, rather than stirred, and can sometimes be served in their own special glass, known as a sours glass.

CHAMBORD SOUR

SERVES 1

whole ice cubes

1 measure Chambord

1 measure rum

1 measure lemon juice

½ egg white

1 tbsp sugar syrup

blackberry, to decorate

1.
Chill a coupe or coupette glass.

2.
Put the ice cubes into a cocktail shaker. Pour the liquid ingredients over the ice cubes.

3.
Shake the cocktail shaker vigorously until the mixture creates foam.

4.
Strain into the chilled coupe glass.

5.
Decorate the cocktail with the blackberry and serve immediately.

CIDER BRANDY SOUR

SERVES 1

1.
Place the ice cubes into a cocktail shaker.

2.
Pour over the cider apple brandy, lemon juice and sugar syrup, then shake thoroughly until well frosted.

3.
Fill a lowball glass with ice cubes. Strain the cocktail into the glass.

4.
Decorate the glass with the lemon slice and serve immediately.

INGREDIENTS

whole ice cubes

2 measures apple brandy

1 measure lemon juice

1 tbsp sugar syrup

lemon slice, to decorate

CHAMPAGNE BITTERS

SERVES 1

1.
Place the sugar cube in the bottom of a chilled champagne flute.

2.
Add the Angostura bitters.

3.
Pour over the brandy.

4.
Top up with champagne and serve immediately.

INGREDIENTS

1 sugar cube

2 tsp Angostura bitters

1 measure brandy

champagne, chilled

SOUR APPLE MARTINI

SERVES 1

1.
Put the cracked ice cubes into a cocktail shaker.

2.
Pour in the vodka, apple schnapps and apple juice.

3.
Shake vigorously until well frosted.

4.
Strain into a chilled martini glass and decorate the glass with the apple wedge. Serve immediately.

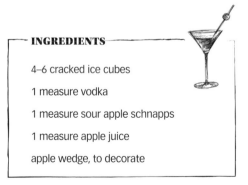

INGREDIENTS

4–6 cracked ice cubes

1 measure vodka

1 measure sour apple schnapps

1 measure apple juice

apple wedge, to decorate

ROB ROY BITTERS

SERVES 1

1.
Chill a coupe glass.

2.
Place the whisky, vermouth, bitters and maraschino syrup into an ice-filled cocktail shaker. Stir with a bar spoon.

3.
Twist the lemon zest over the coupe glass to release its oils and then discard.

4.
Strain the cocktail into the coupe glass.

5.
Decorate the glass with the cherry and serve immediately.

INGREDIENTS

2 measures Scotch whisky

1 measure sweet vermouth

2 tsp Angostura bitters

2 tsp maraschino syrup, from the jar

whole ice cubes

1 piece of lemon zest

maraschino cherry, to decorate

OLD FASHIONED

SERVES 1

1.
Place the sugar cube in a chilled lowball glass.

2.
Add the Angostura bitters and water. Stir until the sugar has dissolved.

3.
Pour in the bourbon and stir.

4.
Add the cracked ice cubes and decorate with the lemon peel. Serve immediately.

INGREDIENTS

1 sugar cube

1 tsp Angostura bitters

1 tsp water

2 measures bourbon or rye whiskey

4–6 cracked ice cubes

lemon peel twist, to decorate

Bitters & Sours

FROZEN RUM SOUR

SERVES 1

1.
Whizz the crushed ice in a blender with the light rum, guava juice, lemon juice and orange juice until it is a slushie consistency.

2.
Pour the frozen mixture into a chilled martini glass.

3.
Serve immediately.

INGREDIENTS

4–6 crushed ice cubes

2 measures light rum

½ measure guava juice

½ measure lemon juice

½ measure orange juice

VIRGIN BITTER GUNNER

SERVES 1

1.
Mix all the ingredients together in a highball glass.

2.
Taste and add more angostura bitters if you wish.

3.
Add the lime slice to the glass and serve immediately.

INGREDIENTS

4–6 ice cubes

50 ml/2 fl oz lime juice

2 tsp Angostura bitters, or to taste

200 ml/7 fl oz ginger beer

200 ml/7 fl oz lemonade

lime slice, to decorate

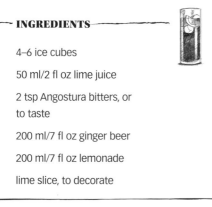

Bitters & Sours

TEQUILA CHERRY COLA

SERVES 1

INGREDIENTS

2 measures tequila

whole ice cubes

½ measure triple sec

½ measure sour cherry syrup

100 ml/3½ fl oz cola

lime wedge, to decorate

TIP
Serve this at a barbecue with tacos or nachos while the barbecue is warming up.

1.
Pour the tequila into an ice-filled lowball glass.

2.
Add the triple sec and sour cherry syrup to the glass.

3.
Top up with the cola.

4.
Decorate with the lime wedge and serve immediately.

CRAFT DECORATION

With really simple cocktails, decoration can be as basic as just adding a single twist of lemon or lime peel to the rim of the glass. But to create some truly beautiful craft cocktails, try experimenting with a range of decoration styles. Botanical cocktails can look great just by adding sprigs of natural herbs in and around the glass, such as thyme sprigs, lemon verbena, mint, lemon balm or fennel fronds, or try decorating with slices or pieces of the natural fruit used in the recipe, such as pomegranate seeds or berries. For decorating with foams and air, see page 13 and for molecular techniques, see page 107.

Another attractive way to add colour and fragrance to cocktails is by using edible flowers or petals. You can use large flowers for a dramatic effect or smaller flowers and petals for a more delicate look or for adding to ice cubes or ice pops. Some popular large edible flowers are coriander flowers, lavender sprigs and flowers, and pansies. Some common small edible flowers are cornflowers, borage, rose petals, elderflowers and violas. Please make sure to always ask for the edible versions of these flowers from your specialist supplier, as not all varieties can be eaten or used in cocktails.

SHERRY, ARMAGNAC & DRAMBUIE BITTERS

SERVES 1

INGREDIENTS

2 measures armagnac

½ measure Amontillado sherry

1 tsp Angostura bitters

½ measure Drambuie

whole ice cubes

orange wedge, to decorate

TIP

This is a classic nightcap or a way to wind down after a big meal at a dinner party.

1.
Pour the Armagnac, sherry, bitters and Drambuie into an ice-filled lowball glass.

2.
Stir with a bar spoon.

3.
Decorate with the wedge of orange and serve immediately.

BOURBON SOUR

SERVES 1

1.
Place the lemon juice, bourbon and sugar into a cocktail shaker filled with ice cubes.

2.
Shake vigorously until well frosted. Strain into a martini glass or sours glass.

3.
Decorate with a slice of orange and serve immediately.

INGREDIENTS

1 measure lemon or lime juice

2 measures bourbon

1 tsp caster sugar

whole ice cubes

orange slice, to decorate

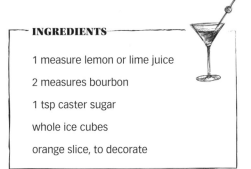

STREGA SOUR

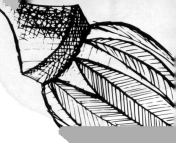

SERVES 1

1.

Place the gin, Strega and lemon juice into a cocktail shaker filled with ice cubes.

2.

Shake vigorously until well frosted. Strain into a martini glass or sours glass.

3.

Decorate with a slice of lemon and serve immediately.

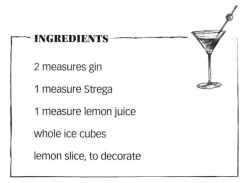

INGREDIENTS

2 measures gin

1 measure Strega

1 measure lemon juice

whole ice cubes

lemon slice, to decorate

BROKEN NEGRONI

SERVES 1

1.
Add the vermouth and bitters to a mixing glass filled with ice and stir.

2.
Strain into a chilled champagne flute.

3.
Top up with sparkling wine and decorate the glass with the orange slice. Serve immediately.

INGREDIENTS

1 measure sweet vermouth

1 measure Campari bitters

whole ice cubes

sparkling wine

half a thin slice of orange, to decorate

Bitters & Sours

WHISKEY SOUR

SERVES 1

1.
Put the cracked ice cubes into a cocktail shaker and pour over the whiskey.

2.
Add the lime juice.

3.
Add the sugar and shake well.

4.
Strain into a martini or wine glass and decorate with the slice of lime and a cherry. Serve immediately.

INGREDIENTS

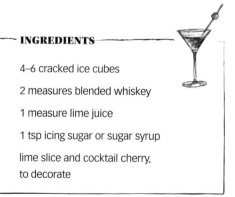

4–6 cracked ice cubes

2 measures blended whiskey

1 measure lime juice

1 tsp icing sugar or sugar syrup

lime slice and cocktail cherry, to decorate

Bitters & Sours

BOSTON SOUR

1.
Place the cracked ice cubes into a cocktail shaker.

2.
Pour over the lemon juice, whiskey and sugar syrup.

3.
Add the egg white. Shake until chilled.

4.
Strain into a martini glass and decorate with the lemon slice and a cocktail cherry. Serve immediately.

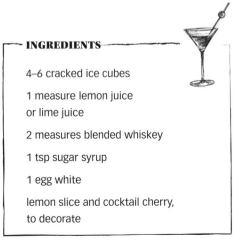

INGREDIENTS

4–6 cracked ice cubes

1 measure lemon juice
or lime juice

2 measures blended whiskey

1 tsp sugar syrup

1 egg white

lemon slice and cocktail cherry,
to decorate

BLOOD ON THE TRACKS

SERVES 1

1.
Pour the bitters into a chilled highball glass filled with ice.

2.
Add the juice. Do not stir.

3.
Top up with sparkling water.

4.
Decorate with the orange slice and mint and serve immediately.

INGREDIENTS

½ measure Campari bitters

whole ice cubes

2½ measures blood orange juice

sparkling water

orange slice and fresh mint sprig, to decorate

INDEX

INDEX - BY COCKTAIL

Honey, Peach & Agave
Infusion 33
Hot Buttered Rum 101

Kimchi & Wasabi Bloody
Mary 88
Kir Royale 105
Klondike Cooler 87

Layered Espresso Shot 97
Lime & Lemon Grass Sling
124

Mandarin & Lime Ginger
Beer 133
Manhattan 61
Margarita 63
Martini 65
Matcha Green Tea Vodka
Refresher 38
Mescal & Watermelon
Foam 108
Midnight Cowboy 134
Mint Julep 137
Mojito 130
Mojito Ice Pops 150
Negroni 100

Old Fashioned 163

Peacemaker Punch 147
Peach & Basil Gin Fix 37
Peach Ice Tea 140
Piña Colada 132
Pink Heather 117
Plum & Ginger Whiskey
Fizz 34
Pomegranate & Mint
Shrub 84

Rattlesnake 113
Rhubarb & Vanilla Bourbon
Cocktail 30
Rob Roy Bitters 162
Rosemary Vodka Cooler 44
Rum Cobbler 66
Rum Cooler 128

Sazerac 118
Sherry, Armagnac &
Drambuie Bitters 170
Sidecar 79
Sour Apple Martini 161
Strawberry Colada 145
Strega Sour 173

Tequila Cherry Cola 166

The Bentley 115
Tom Collins 70
Tricolour 112
Turkish Delight Gin
Cocktail 58

Virgin Bitter Gunner 165
Virgin Collins 77
Virgin Ginger Fizz 96
Virgin Raspberry Coolers
144
Vodka Espresso 94

Whiskey Sangaree 102
Whiskey Sling 62
Whiskey Sour 175
White Russian Blended
Shake 129

INDEX - BY SPIRIT

This edition published by Parragon Books Ltd in 2016

LOVE FOOD is an imprint of Parragon Books Ltd

Parragon Books Ltd

Chartist House

15–17 Trim Street

Bath BA1 1HA, UK

www.parragon.com/lovefood

ISBN 978-1-4748-1747-9

Printed in China

New recipes: Lincoln Jefferson

New and cover photography: Mike Cooper

Designer: Beth Kalynka

Senior Editor: Cheryl Warner

Notes for the Reader

This book uses both metric and imperial measurements. Follow the same units of measurement throughout; do not mix metric and imperial. All spoon measurements are level: teaspoons are assumed to be 5 ml, and tablespoons are assumed to be 15 ml. One measure is assumed to be 25 ml/¾ fl oz. Unless otherwise stated, milk is assumed to be full fat, eggs and individual fruits and vegetables are medium, pepper is freshly ground black pepper and salt is table salt. A pinch of salt is calculated as $1/16$ of a teaspoon. Unless otherwise stated, all root vegetables should be peeled prior to using.

The times given are an approximate guide only. Preparation times differ according to the techniques used by different people and the cooking times may also vary from those given.

Please consume alcohol responsibly.